LET'S LEARN ABOUT MATH

LET'S SUBTRACT

BY CRYSTAL SIKKENS

TABLE OF CONTENTS

A Crabtree Seedlings Book

Crabtree Publishing
crabtreebooks.com

School-to-Home Support for Caregivers and Teachers

This book helps children grow by letting them practice reading. Here are a few guiding questions to help the reader build comprehension skills. Possible answers appear here in red.

Before Reading:

- What do I know about subtraction?
    - *I know subtraction is taking away.*
    - *I know subtraction is taking apart.*
- What do I want to learn about subtraction?
    - *I want to learn how to show things that I am subtracting.*
    - *I want to learn when to use an equal sign.*

During Reading:

- What have I learned so far?
    - *I have learned what a minus sign is.*
    - *I have learned what an equal sign is.*
- I wonder why...
    - *I wonder why we write numbers in an equation.*
    - *I wonder why 6-2 is equal to 4.*

After Reading:

- What did I learn about subtraction?
    - *I have learned that I use an equal sign in an equation to show that both sides are equal.*
    - *I have learned that 10-3=7.*
- Read the book again and look for the glossary words.
    - *I see the word **subtraction** on page 3 and the words **minus sign** on page 4. The other vocabulary words are found on pages 22 and 23.*

I am learning about **subtraction**. Subtraction is taking apart or taking from something.

I use a **minus sign** when I want to subtract.

5 – 2

I use an **equal sign** to show both sides are the same or equal.

5–2=3

When I subtract, I can write the numbers in an **equation**.

equation

minus sign

equal sign

$$6 - 2 = 4$$

I invited 10 friends to my birthday party. Three friends couldn't make it.

How many friends came?

$$10 - 3 = \_$$

Seven friends came to my birthday party!

Ten minus three is seven.

$$10 - 3 = 7$$

My mom cut 11 slices of birthday cake. We ate five slices.

How many slices were left after my party was over?

$$11 - 5 = \_\_\_$$

There were 6 slices of cake left over.

$$11 - 5 = 6$$

I had 14 balloons at my party.
Six balloons popped.

How many balloons are left?

−

$$14 - 6 = \_\_$$

My friend got 20 dollars for her birthday. She spent 15 dollars at the store.

Write an equation that shows how much money she has left.

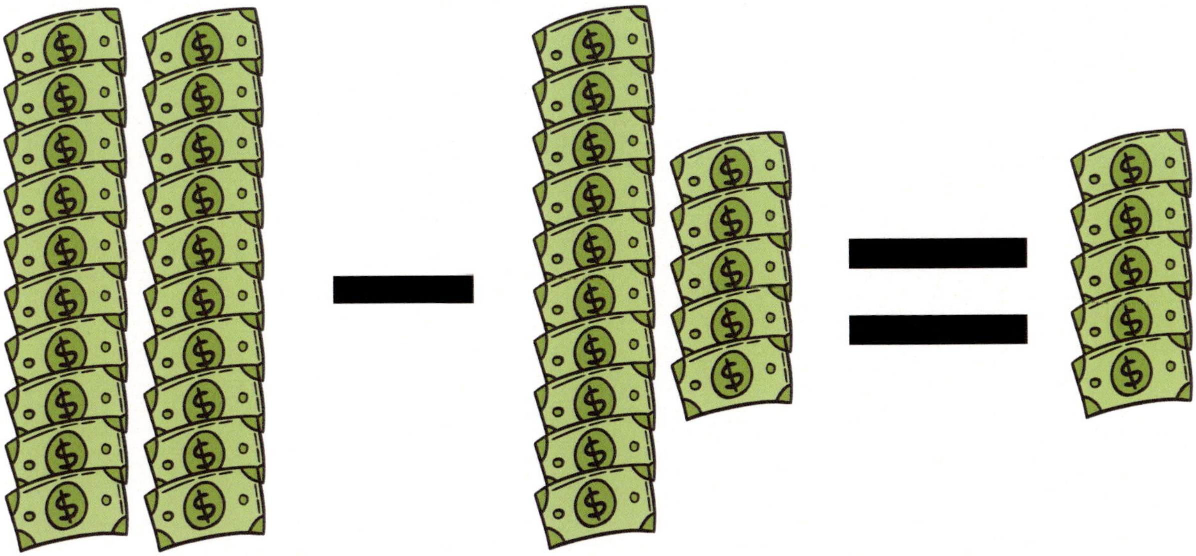

______ − ______ = ______

GLOSSARY

equal sign (e-kwel sain):
A symbol used to show two sides are the same or equal

equation (ih-KWAY-shun):
A math sentence showing two things are equal or the same

minus sign (MY-nus sain):
A symbol used to show subtraction

subtraction (suh-TRAC-shuhn):
To take away from or take apart

INDEX

ABOUT THE AUTHOR

Crystal Sikkens has been helping create books for Crabtree Publishing for over 20 years. In her spare time, she loves spending time with her husband and children on their family farm.

Written by: Crystal Sikkens
Editor: Kathy Middleton
Designed by: Samara Parent
Photographs: All images from Shutterstock
Production manager: Candice Campbell

Crabtree Publishing

crabtreebooks.com 800-387-7650

Hardcover: 978-1-0398-7277-6
Paperback: 978-1-0398-7335-3
Ebook (pdf): 978-1-0398-7391-9
Epub: 978-1-0398-7440-4

Published in Canada
Crabtree Publishing
616 Welland Avenue
St. Catharines, Ontario
L2M 5V6

Published in the United States
Crabtree Publishing
347 Fifth Avenue
Suite 1402-145
New York, New York, 10016

Library and Archives Canada Cataloguing in Publication
Available at Library and Archives Canada

Library of Congress Cataloging-in-Publication Data
Available at the Library of Congress

Printed in the U.S.A./CP032026